WOLF SPIDER
(CARRIES ITS BABIES AROUND ON ITS ABDOMEN)
BIRD
CRAB SPIDER
(HIDES IN PLAIN SIGHT BY LOOKING LIKE BIRD POOP)
(YUCK!)
HAPPY FACE SPIDER
(HAS A HAPPY FACE PATTERN ON ITS BACK—SO CUTE!)
ST. ANDREW'S CROSS SPIDER
(RESTS IN THE SHAPE OF AN "X")
PATU DIGUA SPIDER
(WORLD'S SMALLEST SPIDER!)

T0032986

I'm trying to love spiders.

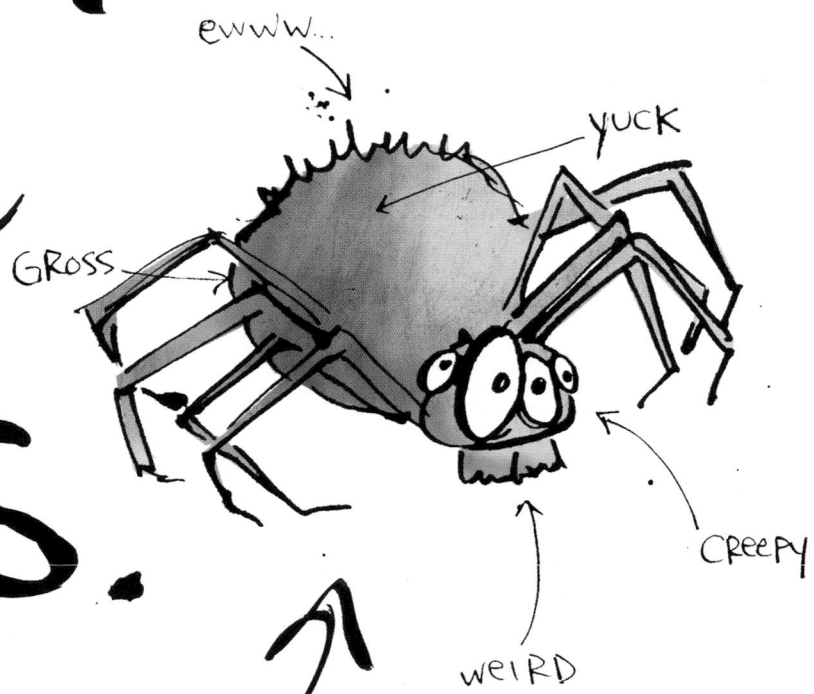

(It isn't easy.)

Words & Pictures by bethany barton

VIKING
An Imprint of Penguin Group (USA)

I KEEP TELLING MYSELF:
"SPIDERS ARE COOL."
I WANT TO LOVE THEM.
ME + SPIDERS 4EVA

I MEAN, SPIDERS HAVE BEEN AROUND FOR MILLIONS OF YEARS.

MOVING SILENTLY.
SWINGING INTO ACTION.

I WANT TO THINK OF THEM LIKE BUG NINJAS...

LIKE THIS SPIDER RIGHT HERE.
I'M GONNA TRY REALLY HARD TO LIKE HIM.
MAYBE IF I STUDY HIM FOR A WHILE...

THINK IT'S WORKING...

AHHHHHH!!

IT'S MOVING!!

SQUISH IT!!

SQUISH IT!!

SQUISH IT!!

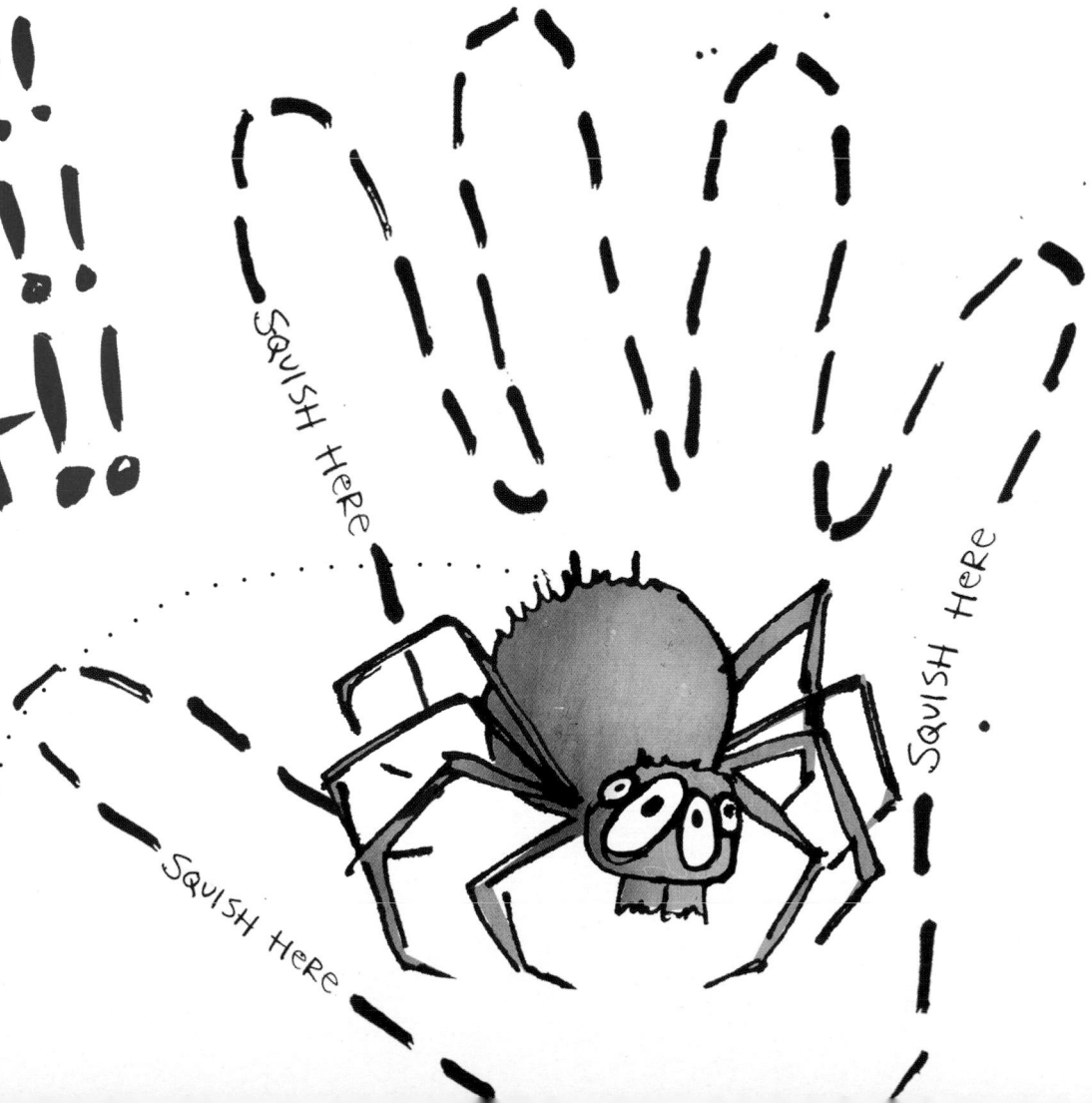

THAT DIDN'T WORK OUT.

BUT NEXT TIME WILL BE BETTER.

Next time I'll focus on all the cool superpowers spiders have.
Like 8 eyes.
Extreme close-up!

AND SPIDERWEBS!
SPIDERWEBS ARE COOL.
FUNNEL WEB
SHEET WEB
SPIRAL ORB WEB
SPIDERS SPIN WEBS OUT OF PROTEIN-PACKED SPIDER SILK THEY MAKE THEMSELVES!

THAT'S LIKE YOU OR ME BUILDING A HOUSE WITH OUR HAIR

AND THEN CATCHING FOOD ON IT.

SOME SPIDERS EVEN HAVE BILLIONS OF TINY HAIRS (CALLED SCOPULAE) ON THEIR LEGS THAT LET THEM STICK ON WALLS OR CEILINGS OR...

OH MY GOSH!
THERE'S A
SPIDER STUCK
ON THERE!
SMASH IT!
SQUISH IT!
GET IT RIGHT NOW!

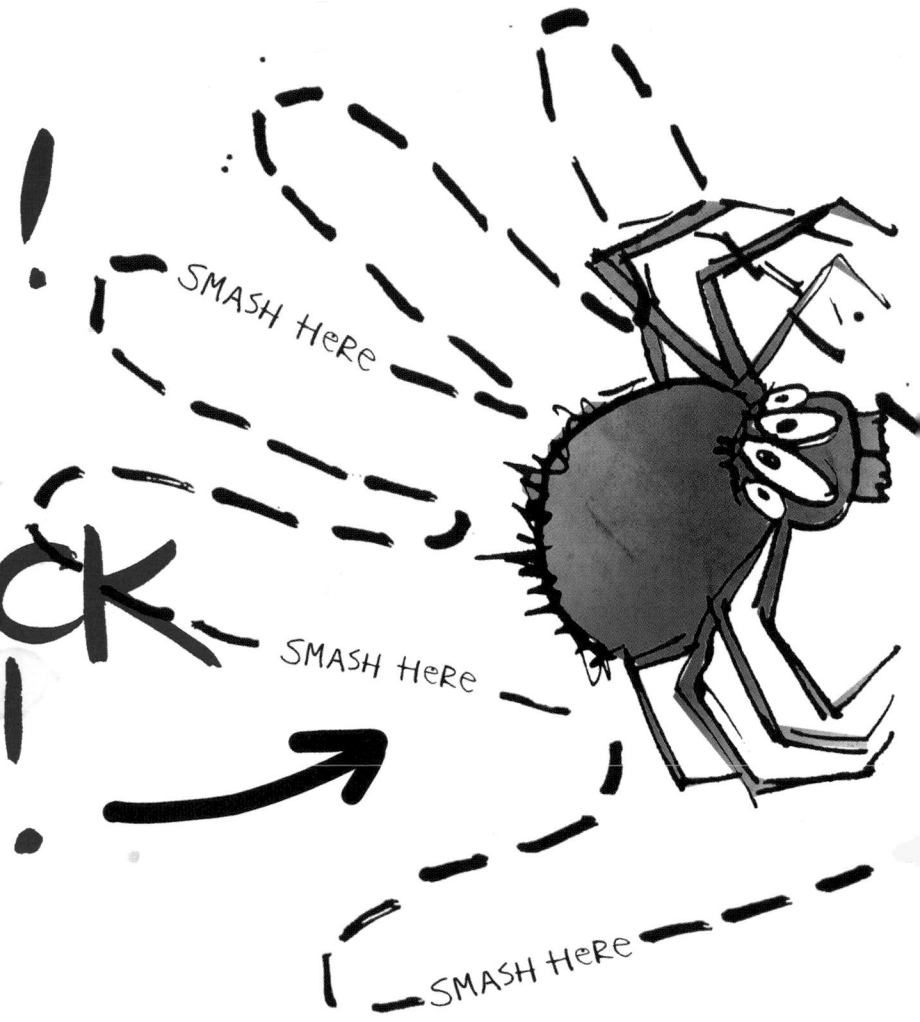

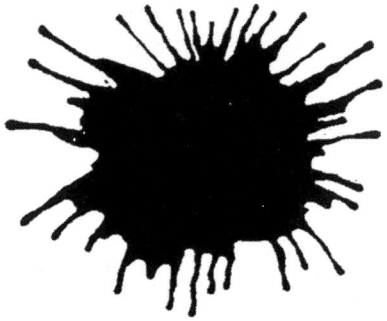

(WE'RE NOT VERY GOOD AT
LOVING SPIDERS JUST YET.)

IF ONLY SPIDERS WERE MORE LIKE THINGS I REALLY LOVE.

INSTEAD THEIR CLOSEST RELATIVES ARE ALSO TOTALLY GROSS.

BUT IT'S NOT LIKE I'M SCARED OF EVERY ICKY THING.

IT'S JUST SOMETHING ABOUT SPIDERS!

MAYBE IT'S THE FACT THAT ALMOST ALL SPIDERS ARE VENOMOUS?

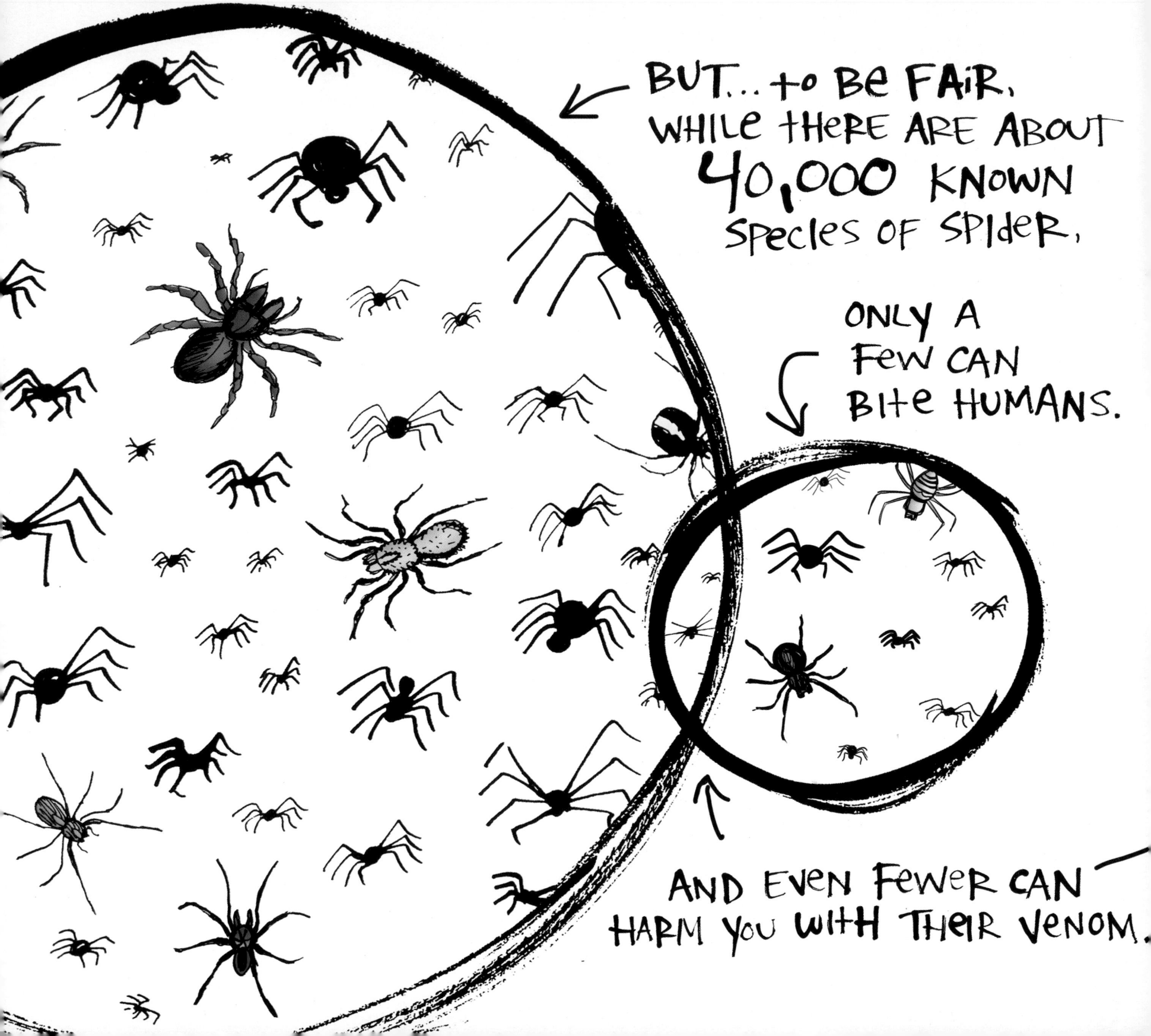
BUT... to be FAIR, WHILE THERE ARE ABOUT 40,000 KNOWN species OF SPIDER,
ONLY A FEW CAN BITE HUMANS.
AND EVEN FEWER CAN HARM YOU WITH THEIR VENOM.

WANTED
DEAD OR SMASHED A LOT
RED HOURGLASS ON UNDERBELLY
VIOLIN-SHAPED MARKING ON ITS BACK
FEMALE BLACK WIDOW
BROWN RECLUSE
FOR BEING POISONOUS ENOUGH TO RUIN YOUR DAY

FATAL SPIDER BITES ARE SO RARE, YOU HAVE A BETTER CHANCE OF GETTING STRUCK BY LIGHTNING!

OH. MY. GOSH.

OKAY, DON'T PANIC...
BUT THERE IS DEFINITELY A SPIDER OVER THERE.

AND WE'RE NOT GONNA SQUISH IT THIS TIME, RIGHT?

WE'LL JUST TRY TO... PET HIM...? MAYBE?

CAN YOU PET SPIDERS?

Let's TRY!

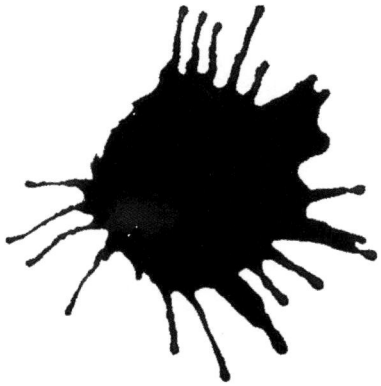

WHOOPS! NOPE.

WE SQUISHED HIM.

I'M NEVER GONNA LOVE SPIDERS AT THIS RATE!!!

MAYBE I SHOULD FOCUS ON WHAT SPIDERS ARE GOOD AT...

LIKE EATING BUGS!

THAT'S GOTTA BE HELPFUL, RIGHT?

A SINGLE SPIDER CAN EAT OVER 75 POUNDS OF BUGS IN A YEAR!

I've even heard that some farmers use spiders to keep harmful insects out of their crops.

AND — OH WAIT...
LOOKS LIKE SOME OF THOSE
BUGS MADE IT OVER HERE...

GET OUT
OF HERE, BUGS!
I CAN'T EVEN READ MY BOOK
WITH ALL THESE...

Hey,
WHAt's tHAt
spider
DOING?

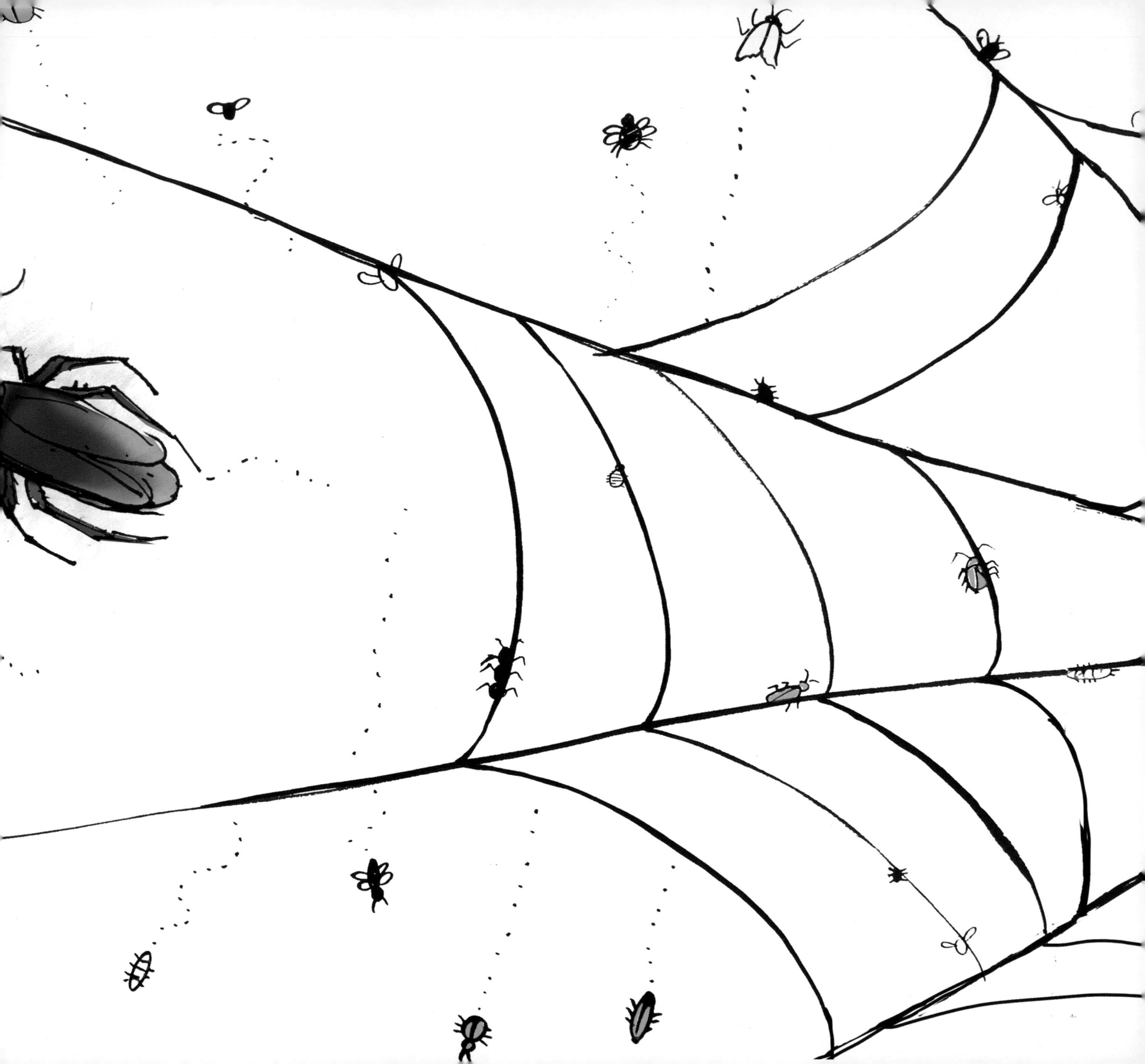

WOW! THANKS, LITTLE GUY! THAT WAS REALLY IMPRESSIVE!

(SPIDER PRESENTS FOR YOU.)

AWW...
DID YOU MAKE THAT FOR ME?
I THINK I MIGHT FINALLY LOVE...

AHHHHH!!
COCKROACH!
SQUISH IT!
SMASH IT!
MAKE IT
GO AWAY!!

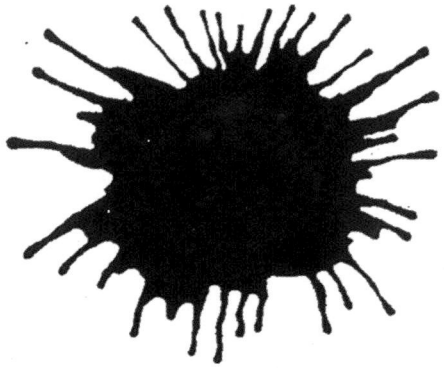

(ONE THING AT A TIME.)

For Leo: The Buddy, The Beastie, My Little Monster

(With a side order of extra thanks to Cindy Barton,
for watching him so I could draw all these spiders.)

VIKING
Published by the Penguin Group
Penguin Group (USA) LLC
375 Hudson Street
New York, New York 10014

USA * Canada * UK * Ireland * Australia
New Zealand * India * South Africa * China

penguin.com
A Penguin Random House Company

First published in the United States of America by Viking, an imprint of Penguin Young Readers Group, 2015

Copyright © 2015 by Bethany Barton

Penguin supports copyright. Copyright fuels creativity, encourages diverse voices, promotes free speech, and creates a vibrant culture. Thank you for buying an authorized edition of this book and for complying with copyright laws by not reproducing, scanning, or distributing any part of it in any form without permission. You are supporting writers and allowing Penguin to continue to publish books for every reader.

LIBRARY OF CONGRESS CATALOGING-IN-PUBLICATION DATA
Barton, Bethany, date- author, illustrator.
I'm trying to love spiders / written and illustrated by Bethany Barton.
pages cm
Summary: "This fresh and very funny non-fiction picture book shares lots of fascinating facts about spiders in an entirely captivating way. If I'm Trying to Love Spiders doesn't cure your spider phobia, it'll at least make you appreciate how amazing they are . . . and laugh a lot as you learn about them."—Provided by publisher.
Audience: Ages 4–8.
Audience: K to grade 3.
ISBN 978-0-670-01693-8 (hardcover)
1. Spiders—Juvenile literature. I. Title. II. Title: I am trying to love spiders.
QL458.4.B365 2015 595.4'4—dc23 2014031680

Manufactured in China

12

The artwork for this book was rendered using inks, paper, computers, and concentrated awesome.
Almost no spiders were harmed in the making of this book.

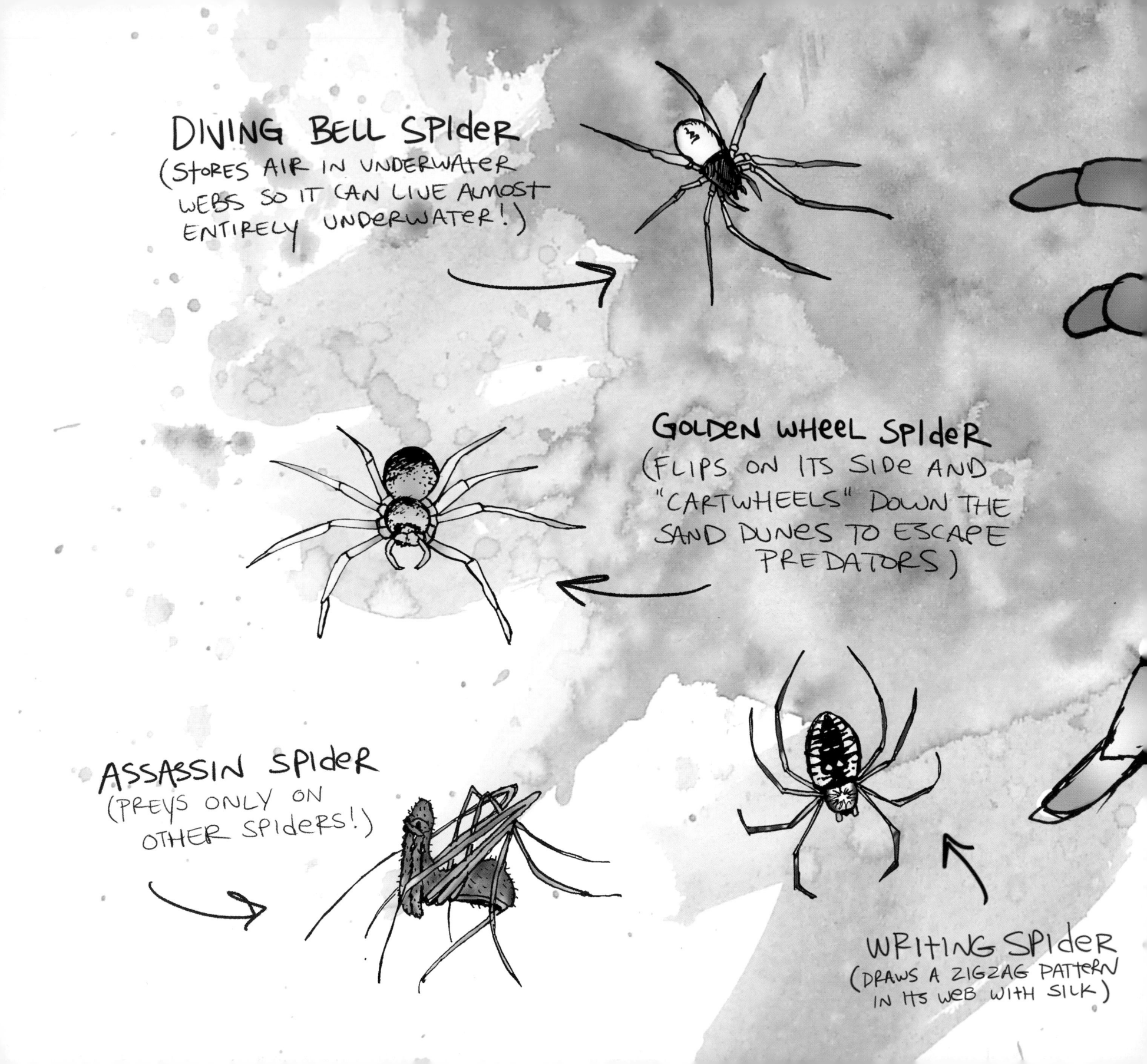
DIVING BELL SPIDER
(STORES AIR IN UNDERWATER WEBS SO IT CAN LIVE ALMOST ENTIRELY UNDERWATER!)
GOLDEN WHEEL SPIDER
(FLIPS ON ITS SIDE AND "CARTWHEELS" DOWN THE SAND DUNES TO ESCAPE PREDATORS)
ASSASSIN SPIDER
(PREYS ONLY ON OTHER SPIDERS!)
WRITING SPIDER
(DRAWS A ZIGZAG PATTERN IN ITS WEB WITH SILK)